Str[a]
Stories of
Glasgow &
the Clyde

Margaret Campbell

Lang**Syne**

PUBLISHING

WRITING *to* REMEMBER

First printed in 1989, reprinted in 2004.
Front cover design: Roy Boyd.

Lang**Syne**

PUBLISHING

WRITING *to* REMEMBER

Strathclyde Business Centre
120 Carstairs Street, Glasgow G40 4JD
Tel: 0141 554 9944 Fax: 0141 554 9955
E-mail: scottishmemories@aol.com
www.scottish-memories.co.uk

© James Barclay
ISBN 1-85217-140-5
Printed by Digi-Source, Livingston

Introduction

What is the wonderful story behind Glasgow's name and why was it known for centuries as 'the dear green place'? What dark secrets from the past are locked inside the city's coat of arms? Who took a stroll across Glasgow Green and suddenly had a brilliant idea that changed the world? When did the massacre of soldiers lead to a bloody battle which was later followed by the burning and looting of the town? Why did the witches want to throw Granny Kempock into the Clyde? Where were 36 members of a family hanged on the same tree? How did icy phantom fingers bring terror to a Glasgow cinema? Who are the pretty ghosts on the 'bluidy stair' and the city Underground? Why was the last man to be hanged in Glasgow a despicable hypocrite?

These fascinating questions, and many more, are answered in Strange Stories of Glasgow and the Clyde, a magical mystery tour of Scotland's most famous city and river.

We start off in Glasgow the hamlet and descriptions from various writers spanning many generations give us a ringside seat of the rapidly changing scene as Glasgow grows and expands. As you would expect in anything connected with the place, there is never a dull moment!

Of course every great city has its river and the Clyde, through shipbuilding, has made Glasgow famous all over the world. In our journey we travel from the Costa resorts 'doon the watter' to high up in the Lanarkshire hills, where the Clyde has its source in the area known as 'God's treasure house in Scotland'.

Find out about the ordeal of a 10-year-old girl cursed by witches who used invisible forces to inflict endless torment; the man freed from a life sentence for murder after investigations by Conan Doyle, the creator of Sherlock Holmes; the sensational case of the lovers and the 'poisoned' cocoa; the day William Wallace, our great Scottish hero, hoodwinked the English and then thrashed them in battle; and the inspiring story of a blind minister who wrote a hymn which today is sung at weddings around the globe.

Other stories tell how a shipwreck gave the Holy Loch its name, why lepers were sent to the Gorbals, why Queen Street was more famous for cows than trains, why dinner guests in a castle were served a meal of gold and silver coins, why a doctor haunts his old hospital, and why toffs who carried gold topped canes were allowed to whack anyone who got in their way.

PLUS many other intriguing yarns!

How St Mungo found his Dear Green Place — and Glasgow flourished!

Glasgow's patron saint had an unfortunate start in life.

According to legend his mother was a Pictish princess, daughter of King Loth of Lothian, who was horrified to find his unwed daughter pregnant.

Since she steadfastly refused to name the father of her unborn infant, she was taken to the top of Traprain Law and thrown off. Unhurt, she picked herself up, only to find her persecutors were not to be deterred in their endeavour to rid themselves of such an embarrassment.

They seized her, flung her into a coracle, pushed it well out into the Firth, and hoped she would be carried out to sea and drowned.

But in the night a wind blew up and the coracle was carried over to the other shore, where the exhausted woman was found by St Serf and gently carried to safety and shelter, where her son Kentigern was born.

St Serf took a great interest in the young boy, giving him the pet name Mungo.

As he grew up his fellow scholars at the Christian community resented the 'teacher's pet' and never missed an opportunity to try and put Mungo in a bad light. But, says legend, Mungo always triumphed, and two of the miracles attributed to this period in his life are commemorated on Glasgow's Coat of Arms.

The boys took it in turns to stay awake at night and tend the fire which was never allowed to die out. One night though, Mungo fell asleep at his post. Some of the other boys found out and quickly doused the flame.

A startled Mungo awoke to find he had failed in the task entrusted to him. But all was not lost. So great was Mungo's faith that he quietly went out into the frosty winter's night and returned carrying a bare frozen twig from a tree.

This he placed on the fire and commanded it to burn. It did — and when the little community awoke the fire was burning as brightly as ever.

Another spiteful attempt to get Mungo into trouble occurred when St Serf's pet robin was killed — and everyone blamed Mungo. But Mungo took the little bird tenderly into his hands

and blessed it, and the robin was immediately as chirpy as ever.

Look closely at Glasgow's Coat of Arms. There you will see a tree and a bird, reminders of only two of the miracles attributed to Mungo's stay at Culross.

But as he grew older Mungo felt called to take the Christian message to another part of the country.

He set off westwards, meaning to spend the night with the hermit Fergus. He arrived to find the saint gravely ill, but able to gasp out his last request. Mungo was to take the body to a resting-place on a cart drawn by two wild bulls — where the bulls stopped, there he must be buried.

Mungo promised to do as the saint commanded. Fergus died in the night.

In the morning, lo and behold, Mungo found two wild bulls roaming nearby ..... but they allowed themselves to be rounded up and yoked to the saint's cart.

Off they set westwards and when they stopped Mungo found they were near a burn. There he buried Fergus — and found the saint's resting-place was in ground consecrated as a Christian burial-ground some two hundred years earlier by St Ninian.

Here, young Mungo decided, was an idyllic place to begin his ministry.

There was work a-plenty for him to do. The handful of Christians in the area welcomed an energetic enthusiastic Christian crusader who would lead them in the faith.

One version of the legend says Mungo named his new home 'Glas Ghu' — the 'dear green place', and from this, 'Glasgow' is derived.

Soon there gathered around Mungo a little community. A monastery was founded. The faithful had to have some means of knowing when to attend worship. The bell on Glasgow's Coat of Arms represents the bell used by Mungo for this and given to him, according to one version, by a fellow bishop when Mungo himself was persuaded to accept the bishopric of the community which had grown under his ministry.

Another version tells of Mungo making a pilgrimage to Rome and there receiving from the Pope himself a gift of a bell for the comparatively new community.

When Mungo returned, so the story goes, he gave a glowing account of his travels to his brethren, and prayed, 'Let Glas Ghu flourish by the preaching of Thy word and praising Thy name.' Glasgow's motto, incorporated in its Coat of Arms, is an abbreviated version — 'Let Glasgow Flourish.'

But in the secular world around Glas Ghu men of power strove for supremacy. At one time Morken triumphed. He was an evil cruel heathen king who hated Mungo. So great was his enmity and persecution that Mungo was forced to leave his 'dear green place' and become a wandering missionary for some years in Cumbria and Wales.

Better days dawned however when Morken was defeated and the Christian king Rydderch retook his kingdom.

Mungo was invited to return to 'Glas Ghu', and to this part of his life we owe the legend of the fish on Glasgow's Coat of Arms.

The king, Rydderch, had a beautiful wife, Queen Languoreth, who became infatuated with one of her husband's courtiers. Rather imprudently she bestowed upon him a ring .... but it was a ring given to her in love by her husband.

No doubt she hoped that the one item missing from her jewellery collection would never be missed by her husband.

Alas it was! And he knew where it had gone!

But rather than confront her with her indiscretion he contrived to relieve the courtier of the ring while he slept by the riverside. Then he flung it into the river.

Next day the king asked his wife to wear the ring.

Languoreth decided all she had to do was to ask her lover if she could borrow it back for a day. Then the courtier claimed he had no idea where it was!

Look carefully at the fish on Glasgow's Coat of Arms — in its mouth you will see a ring.

Mungo ended his days preaching the Word of God all around the area. He died in the early years of the 7th century and was buried near his beloved Molendinar Burn, in the consecrated ground where, so many years earlier, he had buried Fergus.

Centuries later a Cathedral was built and dedicated to the memory of St Mungo. Glasgow Cathedral today stands on the same site and, in its oldest part, is St Mungo's tomb. And if you look carefully at the nearby stonework you will see a carving of two bulls drawing a cart on which lies the body of Fergus, whose burial led to St Mungo settling in the Glas Ghu area.

His stroll across Glasgow Green changed the world!

Mention a village green and a picture is formed in the mind of an expanse of grass-covered land in the middle of a small group of houses — well, Glasgow too has its 'green', but, in keeping with the size of the city, 'Glasgow Green' covers around 150 acres, with the River Clyde as its southern boundary. The 'Green' is certainly the oldest public park in Glasgow, and in Britain too. And there are those who claim it is the oldest public park in Europe!

Near the western entrance is Jocelyn Square, named after Jocelyn, the 12th century bishop who was responsible for organising the building of Glasgow Cathedral after the original, dedicated in 1136, was destroyed by fire. The Cathedral stands on St Mungo's burial-ground, that piece of land that was consecrated ground two centuries even before Mungo's time. Jocelyn Square was originally called 'Jail Square' and crowds used to congregate at Glasgow Green to watch public executions in the square across the road. But when the prison was demolished it was felt expedient to change the name of the square, hoping that the memory of the spectacles once afforded the public would be dimmed with time.

Bishop Jocelyn did well for the general public during his years in office, for he is also credited with petitioning the King to have Glasgow upgraded to a 'burgh', and, to the even greater joy of Glaswegians, obtained a Royal Charter to hold an annual fair. The Fair was held on common land, once the forested Bishop's land, but now part of Glasgow Green, and over the centuries, the entertainments expanded to cover more and more of the land, and Bishop Jocelyn's 'Fair' is still held as the annual fortnight's holiday in Glasgow — though nowadays, of course, more and more Glaswegians seek their pleasures elsewhere! But for stay-at-homes there is still entertainment on

Glasgow Green at the Fair, even if it is not now so large as in days of yore.

Glaswegians love to claim to be 'first' with things, and on Glasgow Green, they claim, was the first golf course in the town ..... and, of course, the first in Scotland!

Don't run away with the idea that Glasgow Green was wholly given over to leisure pursuits — oh no, part of the Green was also used as a 'drying-green' where ordinary women would bring their clothes to dry having done their week's washing at a near-by 'public wash-house', and mingling with them would be servants from the 'toffs' houses that overlooked the Green.

To Glaswegians the 'Green' has been the meeting-place whenever they felt they needed to congregate together. At first to enjoy themselves at the 'Fair', then just to stroll and listen to anyone who wanted to get on his 'soap-box' and expound his theories and opinions to any who would hear him. Lovers would do their courting there. And wherever people met in great numbers was the right place to be, thought the 19th century evangelists Moody and Sankey, who conducted their very successful evangelical campaign in a tent on Glasgow Green. So great was the response they got that a more permanent building was erected nearby and named the 'Tent' Hall, for years the venue of many a religious rally.

Where else but on Glasgow Green would troops muster? Glaswegians may not have been too enthralled when Bonnie Prince Charlie visited their city with his supporters, but they did take a keen interest in Napoleon's endeavours to conquer Europe. After all, it was a 'local laddie', Sir John Moore, who died a hero in the Peninsular War. Does the name seem vaguely familiar to you? An older generation will remember:

'Not a drum was heard, not a funeral note,
As his corpse to the ramparts we hurried:
Not a soldier discharged a farewell shot
O'er the grave where our hero we buried.'

So when volunteers were wanted to form a local regiment Glasgow men were proud to join up.

Glasgow also prides itself on being the first town with a monument erected to another of Napoleon's adversaries. On Glasgow Green stands the Nelson Monument.

James Watt gets the idea while crossing Glasgow Green

During the last quarter of the 19th century other 'reviews of local troops were held on the Green, one especially going down in history as the 'wet review', when the weather was so bad that quite a few of those who enlisted to fight to the death for Queen and country did die — but as a result of catching pneumonia.

Not all those who mustered on Glasgow Green were orderly for on a number of occasions the crowd turned into a rioting mob. Along with many other cities and towns all over Europe, in 1848, the Year of the Revolutions, Glasgow had its subversives encouraging the mob to riot and demand their rights. Where did they meet? On Glasgow Green of course!

Forget the story we were told at school of James Watt sitting in his mother's kitchen watching the steam coming from a kettle and realising that if a small amount of steam could move the lid, then a great amount of steam could probably move a heavier object, and so he went on to invent the steam engine. Not so, not so. He himself says he got the idea one day while he was walking across Glasgow Green. And if you have any doubts about it, just go to Glasgow Green, make your way to Nelson's Monument, look around for a huge stone nearby, and there read its inscription: 'Near this spot in 1765 James Watt conceived the idea of the separate condenser for the steam engine, patented 1769.'

James Watt was born in Greenock, further down the Clyde, but Glasgow takes pride in the fact that he was living in Glasgow, working at the University, when he had his marvellous idea.

What the English King's spy wrote about Glasgow

Glasgow at one time was a salmon-fishing village. And so plentiful was herring in the Clyde that they were used as part-payment for wages!

It was chosen as a most suitable place for a University in 1451 because 'the air is mild, victuals are plentiful', and it was 'a place of renown'.

Visitors in the 15th, 16th and 17th centuries had been very complimentary about the city.

John Hardyng was an Englishman sent by Henry V to Scotland ostensibly in search of some papers that were supposed to confirm the superiority of England.

Henry had tentative plans to take over Scotland.

For three and a half years Hardyng travelled around, taking note of the distances between towns and observing the state of the country, reporting back to his King 'ye waye how to conveigh an armie as well as by lande as water, into the chiefest parts thereof.'

Henry's plans came to nought, however, for he had other matters demanding his attention other than an invasion of Scotland, but years later Hardyng wrote an account of his travels in a book.

His description of Glasgow will delight Glaswegians:—

'Next than from Ayre unto Glasgow go,
A goodly cytee and universitee,
Wherre plentifull is the countree also,
Replenished well with all commoditee:'

Hardyng suggested that three separate armies should converge on Glasgow:

'The thyrde army from Barwyke passe it shall ....'
(via Dunbar, Edinburgh, Linlithgow and Stirling)
'And nexte from that unto Glasgo
Standyng upon Clyde, and where also
Of corne and cattell is aboundance
Youre armye to vittayle at all suffyaunce.'

In the first half of the 17th century Sir William Brereton wrote his account of his visit to Glasgow:

'.... about 20,000 persons in the town, which is famous for the church, which is fairest and stateliest in Scotland, for the toll-boothe and bridge.'

When Thomas Tucker was sent to Scotland by Cromwell in 1655 to help set up customs and excise posts, of the eight main trading towns selected, Glasgow was one of only two on the West coast.

Reporting on his travels he says that after venturing into the Western Isles he will: 'Returne southerly as farre as Glasgowe, a very neate burgh towne lyeing upon the bankes of the River Clyde .... this towne, seated in a pleasant and fruitfull soyle .... is one of the most considerablest burghs in Scotland, as well for structure as trade of it.'

Contemporary with Thomas Tucker was Richard Franck, who, during a tour of duty in Scotland as one of Cromwell's troopers, found its rivers and lochs ideal for his favourite pastime — angling.

Eagerly he returned North as a civilian, and in between days spent fishing, wrote down his impressions of Scotland. Of Glasgow he wrote :

'The splendor and gaity of this city of Glasgow which surpasseth most, if not all the corporations in Scotland.'

Of its Tolbooth he said: 'Infinitely excelling the model and usual built of town-halls, and is without exception, the paragon of beauty in the West ....'

He enthused over the well-stocked warehouses with a large variety of home and foreign goods: praised the 'flourishing city' where 'streets and channels are so cleanly swept' and 'the people were decently drest.' (He rather spoils things though by finding so much good to say of it that he is compelled to regard it as 'an emblem of England'!)

Still another traveller of the same era was Jorevin de Rocheford who visited Scotland in 1661. He writes:

'The streets of Glasgow are large and handsome, as if belonging to a new town.' On his conducted tour of the city he saw as part of the College, 'A large and very fine garden, filled with all kinds of fruit-trees, deemed scarce in that country.'

James Brome, a Church of England clergyman, in 1669 says he came to 'The renowned city of Glasgow .... and for pleasantness of sight, sweetness of air, and delightfulness of its gardens and orchards enriched with the most delicious fruits, surpasseth all other places in this tract.'

Another gentleman of the cloth, the Rev Thomas Morer, was Chaplain to a Scottish regiment.

His account of his Scottish travels in 1689 mentions: 'Glasgow is a place of great extent and good situation; and has the reputation of the finest town in Scotland, not excepting Edinburgh ....'

In 1723 Daniel Defoe (of Robinson Crusoe fame) in 'A Journey Through Scotland' said of Glasgow:

'The beautifullest litle city I have seen in Britain.'

Tobias Smollett in the 18th century wrote:

'I am so far happy as to have seen Glasgow, which to the best of my recollection and judgment is one of the prettiest towns in Europe; and, without all doubt, it is one of the most flourishing in Great Britain.'

Alas, all these travellers wrote of Glasgow as they found it — prior to the Industrial Revolution.

Mention 'Glasgow' earlier in this century and people would shudder, for 'Glasgow', to the stranger who had never been there, was synonymous with squalid slums, dirt, poverty, industrial smoke and violence.

Only now as a determined effort is being made to rid Glasgow of its bad image, are outsiders learning that Glasgow is a great place to visit, and visitors, discovering all Glasgow has to offer, decide to return again — and again.

No tale of Glasgow would be complete without mentioning its great rival — Edinburgh.

For years the cities have enjoyed a feud, and 'enjoyed' is the right word, for there is nothing malicious or nasty in the rivalry.

Rather do the inhabitants of both places find great joy in poking fun at each other. A well-quoted saying of Glasgow comics is 'The best thing ever to come out of Edinburgh? The Glasgow train from Waverley Station!' (It's still heard from time to time on some Scottish programmes on television!)

And when folk in Edinburgh get a bit above themselves and talk 'wi a bool in their moo' of being 'The Capital', the folk in Glasgow drily remind them, 'Aye, Edinburgh might **be** the Capital, but Glesca **has** the Capital!'

Even in fiction the contrast between Glasgow and Edinburgh is drawn.

John Buchan's sister Anna, writing as O.Douglas in Penny Plain, tells a story of an impoverished young girl living in Priorsford (Peebles) in the years just after the First World War.

She is left a fortune by an eccentric old man who has been so busy making his fortune he had no time to make friends.

Jean is kind to him, thinking him poor and sick, and is astonished when she is left all his money.

Two of the other characters in the book are talking about Jean's expeditions to Edinburgh and Glasgow to stock her wardrobe.

Lady Pamela, a visitor to the village who is spending a few months in lodgings there next door to Jean and has made friends with her, is describing to Mrs Hope, a family friend, just how difficult it had been to persuade Jean to go to the cities for shopping, but in the end thay had gone first to Edinburgh. It was Lady Pamela's first visit to Edinburgh ....

'And weren't you charmed? Edinburgh is our town, and we are inordinately proud of it ....'

'It's a fairy-tale place to see', Pamela said .... 'but Glasgow — — ' 'I know almost nothing of Glasgow' said Mrs Hope, 'But I like the people that come from it. They are not so devoured by gentility as our Edinburgh friends ....'

After a discussion on the 'gentility' of Edinburgh, Lady Pamela goes on to say, 'Jean and I were much interested in the difference between Edinburgh and Glasgow shops.'

They had found the Glasgow shop assistants not nearly so frightening as their Edinburgh counterparts! In the manner of selling Glasgow won hands down.

They had taken great interest in the purchases made, recommending them and passing comments on how Jean looked in various items; so much so that she had bought a lot more than she had intended!

So even in fiction the rivalry is depicted!

Edinburgh's citizens pride themselves on their gentility and culture — but Glasgow claims to be friendlier and warmer-hearted. (Only a light-hearted controversy this, though, as, on the quiet, citizens of both towns acknowledge that there is a goodly mixture of all these qualities to be found in **both** places.)

Bloodshed at Langside and a ransom for the Jacobites

James I of Scotland didn't think highly of his ancestor King David I — he called him 'a sair sanct for the croon', it is said.

David had been very generous in giving lands to the Church, and it was he who decided that a Cathedral should be built in Glasgow in memory of St Mungo.

Before he succeeded his brother as king, David had been Prince of Strathclyde and was well acquainted with the area, taking a particular interest in its religious history.

It was this Cathdedral which was burned to the ground just a few years after it was finished in 1136.

David's grandson, William the Lyon, granted permission to Bishop Jocelyn for a fair to be held in 1189, and annually, so when Glasgow folk go on holiday in the last fortnight of July, they are enjoying a break that has been an institution for 800 years!

Glasgow found itself embroiled in one or two minor skirmishes in the early days of the 'rough wooing' when Henry VIII seemed set on forcing a marriage between his sickly son and the infant Mary, Queen of Scots. She was only a few months old when he was proposing she should be taken to England and prepared for a marriage to unite the two countries!

He went too far though when he demanded not only custody of the infant queen but that English soldiers should garrison some of Scotland's strongholds!

It is said that the Provost of Edinburgh drily remarked to the English Ambassador, 'If your lad were a lass, and our lass was a lad, would you then be so earnest in this matter? And could you be content that our lad should marry your lass, and so be King of England?'

When the Ambassador earnestly assured him that he would be agreeable if it were for the good of the nation, the Provost retorted, 'Well, if you had the lass, and we had the lad, we could well be contented with it.'

The Provost then went on to make the Ambassador aware in no uncertain terms that even if the nobility agreed, the common people would rise up against it.

But to Henry's proposal some of the nobility did agree, of course, and some disagreed. And the opening rounds of the disagreement took place in Glasgow.

Mary Queen of Scots at the Battle of Langside

Two powerful men each thought they should be Regent —
the Earl of Arran (a Hamilton), and the Earl of Lennox (a
Stewart); and each had his supporters.

Lennox's men occupied the Bishop's Castle in Glasgow.
Arran beseiged it.

For ten days Lennox's men held out, then, on the promise
by Arran of mercy, they surrendered.

Arran massacred them as they left the Bishop's Castle.
Only two escaped — to carry news of the disgraceful treachery
to Lennox, who immediately enlisted the aid of the Earl of
Glencairn and his troops and marched to meet Arran's
army.

They met on Gallowmuir, where Glasgow executed its
criminals at one time.

Arran won. So enraged was he that the citizens of Glasgow had supported Lennox and Glencairn that he ransacked the town, plundering and pillaging, looting and burning. That affray went down in history as the Battle of the Butts (1544)

Arran vacillated between supporting the union with England, and the union with France, favoured by the baby queen's mother.

But over the next year or two Henry rampaged so much in sending 'invasions' of troops that even those who supported union with England were so disgusted at the 'rough wooing' that they too turned against him, and little Mary, now five years old, was sent off for safety to France and marriage with the Dauphin.

By the time she returned to Scotland in 1561 she was a 19-year-old widow.

Crookston Castle, the ruins of which now stand in the middle of a Glasgow housing estate, belonged at that time to the Earl of Lennox (he who had claimed to be Regent in her babyhood), and here, according to tradition, Mary and Lennox's son, Henry Darnley, courted and spent part of their honeymoon in 1565.

Wedded bliss didn't last long however. Mary was soon disillusioned.

She visited Darnley in Glasgow where he was lying sick in one of the Darnley homes in Duke Place.

The Queen stayed in Provand's Lordship (now, as the oldest house in Glasgow, a museum, and quite near to the Cathedral), and here, if the 'casket letters' are genuine, was where she wrote them, implicating herself in the plot to get rid of Darnley.

From Glasgow, a week later, she took her convalescing husband back to Edinburgh — and death by murder.

Two years later Mary was back in Glasgow, en route via Craignethan and Cadzow Castles (after her escape from Loch Leven) to Dumbarton Castle.

Her supporters met up with her enemies at Langside where Mary's army was soundly beaten. Glasgow supported Mary's enemies — because Arran, who had pillaged and burnt their town 20 years earlier, was on Mary's side — and the Glaswegians had neither forgiven nor forgotten.

All around this area are reminders of the battle — Battlefield Road, Queen's Park, Battle Place ..... and of course the site from which Mary is said to have watched the battle is marked by a stone.

By the time of the 1715 Jacobite rebellion the merchants of Glasgow were beginning to realise how they were benefiting by the union with England and the increased trade with her colonies that was open to them, so they were definitely pro-Hanoverian. Not only did they donate money for King George, but they raised a regiment to fight for him!

Thirty years later they were no more enamoured of the Old Chevalier's son, Bonnie Prince Charlie.

When he was making his victorious way south via Edinburgh in 1745 he demanded that Glasgow should forward £15,000 towards his campaign expenses. Glasgow Town Council ignored him, thinking he didn't stand much chance of victory.

But everything seemed to be going in the Prince's favour, so rather reluctantly they sent £5,000 when a second demand came — and they breathed a sigh of relief when the Jacobites marched into England. A few months later they heard that the Prince and his army were in retreat — and their route lay through Glasgow. But Glasgow had again raised troops and sent them to fight for the government!

The Jacobite retreat from Derby had led to much of their equipment being abandoned en route north — so when they arrived in Glasgow all tattered, the Prince decided it was time to replenish his army — and that Glasgow, who hadn't contributed as much as he thought they should to his cause, should foot the bill!

He demanded: 12,000 shirts, 6,000 short coats, 6,000 pairs of shoes, 6,000 bonnets (blue), and 6,000 pairs of stockings ..... and when as much as possible of the demand had been met, the Highlanders, wearing their new finery, were mustered and inspected on Flesher's Haugh, now part of Glasgow Green. Very few Glaswegians turned out to see the sight!

A demand for clothes

Glasgow's coldness to his cause enraged Bonnie Prince Charlie. A story is told that some of the Highlanders proposed ransacking and burning Glasgow as a reprisal for its anti-Jacobite sentiments, but the Prince was persuaded by Cameron of Lochiel not to allow such an ugly revenge which would only alienate the citizens more.

The anxious Town Councillors were so grateful to Lochiel when the Prince took his advice that they vowed that whenever a Cameron of Lochiel came to Glasgow the bells of the Tolbooth would be rung in welcome.

Bonnie Prince Charlie commandeered Shawfield Mansion, the most elegant house he could find in the city — but his prestigious address brought him no callers except for a few impressionable young ladies, among them Clementine Walkinshaw, daughter of a Glasgow laird. She fell for his charms and it was no passing fancy, for after his defeat at Culloden and consequent flight to the continent, the young Glasgow lassie joined her royal lover in exile and shared all his hardships until her Prince died.

The Jacobites marched out of Glasgow ten days after they entered it — and as the Glaswegians hadn't quite managed to furnish all the Prince's demands they took with them two hostages, Archibald Coates and George Carmichael.

That was the last Glasgow saw of Bonnie Prince Charlie — but in 1749 the two hostages were compensated by a small payment for their enforced march, and Glasgow was reimbursed £10,000 for what had been extracted from them to finance and equip the Jacobites!

William Wallace and the battle at Bell o' the Brae

One of Scotland's great heroes is William Wallace.
Generations of Scottish schoolchildren have thrilled to tales of his exploits against the English.

Suddenly the fleeing mob turned . . . .

Since he was a native of the area, having been born in Elderslie near Paisley, his earliest sorties against the enemy were concentrated around the South-West, and on two or more occasions skirmishes occurred in Glasgow.

One especially remembered was 'the Battle o' Bell o' the Brae'.

Near Glasgow Cathedral, on the site now occupied by the Royal Infirmary, stood the Bishop's Castle.

King Edward of England didn't take too kindly to the Bishop of Glasgow allying himself with the Scottish resistance movement, so he had the Bishop carted off to prison, and installed his own supporters as a garrison under the command of the warrior Bishop Beck of Durham.

They thought they had Glasgow and the surrounding countryside well subdued — and sallied forth contemptuously to deal with a small guerilla band that seemed to be asking for trouble in the nearby High Street.

It wasn't long before the would-be attackers were fleeing, hotly pursued by a confident English force.

Then suddenly the fleeing mob turned, battle was joined — and the over-confident enemy found they had been outwitted.

and the enemy found they had been outwitted

Wallace had attacked and drawn the pursuit with only half his force — the other half advanced on the rear of the now beleaguered garrison.

Wallace's victory at Bell o' the Brae may have been a minor one, but it gave a much needed boost to Scottish morale.

Walk across Victoria Bridge, built in the middle of the 19th century and you are crossing the spot where the Romans forded the river, and where the first stone bridge, built in the mid-14th century stood (with some repairs and renovations) for 500 years until it was demolished and replaced with the renamed 'Victoria' Bridge.

Before the old Glasgow Bridge was built, a wooden structure had carried travellers over the Clyde since the days of Mungo's ministry, and Wallace and his followers had made good their escape over it on at least one occasion after a revengeful harrying of the English forces.

Leading down to the bridge is one of the oldest streets in Glasgow — Stockwell Street, and, according to legend, it features in one of Wallace's exploits.

Again a successful attack on the enemy had left quite a few corpses lying around. Before they rode off to a safe hiding-place Wallace decided to tidy up.He ordered his men to get rid of the bodies by throwing them in the well in the middle of the street.

The well is no longer there, of course, but for the years it remained its waters were shunned as being undrinkable — polluted with all the Sassenach bodies stuffed into it!

Riddle of the spirit 'seeking Justice?'

A city as old as Glasgow has to have its quota of ghosts.

One apparition, reported on numerous occasions, haunted the banks of the Clyde in the area around Glasgow Green and Hutcheson Street.

Sometimes she appeared to be an ordinary woman bowed down with care, at other times she assumed gigantic proportions, her appearance terrifying, and seemingly intent on making her desire for revenge apparent.

No one knew who she was, or what her distress, until a man came forward with an extraordinary story.

A few months earlier, one dark autumn evening, he had been making his way home along the Gallowgate when he heard the terrified shrieks of a woman.

The man stopped. Overhead a window opened: the shrieks grew louder. Suddenly a body plummeted down from above his head.

He stood petrified, but just as he was plucking up courage to approach the broken bundle that lay in the street, a group of men clattered down the close and surrounded the fall victim.

One of them bent down, then swore savagely as he muttered, 'She's not dead, she's not dead!'

The onlooker silently drew further back into the shadows as the cursing gang beat the life out of their victim. Satisfied that she was now dead, they dragged her body off in the direction of the river where a new bridge was being built.

The onlooker confessed he had been too terrified to follow, and too scared to tell anyone of his experience until he heard of the apparition that had taken to manifesting itself in the area.

He could only conclude that the poor woman's body had been disposed of in the foundations of the new bridge, as no body had ever been found in the river.

Everyone who heard his story agreed that it must be the ghost of the woman, so cruelly murdered, who was haunting the area, hoping that someone would pay attention and look into her death, then try to bring her murderers to justice.

But of all those who saw her no one was brave enough to linger near to learn the full story.

Tragic secret of the phantom hand and case of baby saved by ghost!

Some ghosts have the knack of seeking out people with whom they wish to communicate, no matter where thay are. Never mind that the place is unfamiliar to the ghost, it is the **person** who matters.

Like the Govan woman who sat enjoying the film showing in one of Glasgow's cinemas. Suddenly she felt icy fingers touch her cheek. She glared round at the folk in the seats behind, but they were all engrossed in the picture.

Rather crossly she complained to her husband when she got home — only to find him looking at her rather strangely. He questioned her closely about her experience, and seemed worried.

When they went to bed that night she heard him give a muffled exclamation. She followed his gaze to the window. How strange!

She could almost swear she could see a delicate-looking, well-cared for hand pressing against the window.

Her husband hurried over and grabbed the hand, but as he held on it disintegrated and he was left grasping nothing!

The woman trembled as her husband led her to the kitchen. A cup of tea was just what was needed to steady her nerves.

As they drank he told her haltingly of a legend in his family which said that whenever that particular branch of his clan was to endure sorrow, a phantom hand appeared. He was convinced that they were to receive bad news.

Next morning word came that the wife's brother had died.

One ghost came all the way from America to rendezvous with his brother who was staying for a few days in a Glasgow hotel.

The brother, an actor, decided to pamper himself while he was appearing in the city. Instead of the usual sleazy digs, he would treat himself to a few nights in a respectable hotel.

But before long he was wishing he hadn't been so good to himself, for he had the most horrifying nightmares. He never had a decent night's sleep. He blamed the food he was eating at supper-time.

On the fourth night he was soon fast asleep, only to be wakened by a tremendous crash.

He got out of bed, but then couldn't find it again. As he stumbled around the room he felt something brush against his head. He looked up.

A noose was hanging in the air! He lashed out, but the swinging noose gradually came lower and lower until it settled over his neck.

Try as he might, he couldn't free himself. He felt himself choking and passed out.

When he came to himself he was lying on the bedroom floor. A nightmare to surpass all nightmares, he told himself.

Next morning the room looked quite normal; but all that day how he dreaded having to go back to that bedroom.

Wearily he made his way to bed that night determined to leave a candle burning till daybreak.

He fell fast asleep. An hour or two later he suddenly woke up and found the room in darkness. As he turned to grope for the matches he touched something cold and flabby in the bed beside him.

He rolled away as fast as he could and fell on to the floor. As his eyes became accustomed to the darkness he began to make out the outline of the furniture. There **was** someone else in his bed!

He started to tremble. But his fear turned to astonishment as he recognised his own brother, who was supposed to be in America.

Even as he gaped a change came over the occupant of the bed. His face became distorted in agony and he gasped and choked.

'I have been wanting to speak to you .... cannot explain, something prevented me .... I have been dead for a month: not cancer .... poison .... Dolly .... poison ....' Then all was quiet. The bed was empty.

Next day the actor received word that his brother in America had died of cancer of the throat.

Still another ghost was desperate to communicate with the young married couple who had so happily moved with their baby into a council flat.

But the ghost only succeeded in terrifying them as it sought to attract their attention by banging and crashing about and moving furniture. The couple fled to relatives for peace and quiet and normality.

Word got round of their strange experience and a group interested in such happenings volunteered to stay overnight in the flat.

On their second visit they too heard crashes and saw furniture move, but no ghost. They decided it must be a spirit anxious to get in touch with the living — but not succeeding very well.

An expert was required. A medium was asked along to see if he was any more successful in establishing contact.

That night as they sat quietly waiting, the medium suddenly went into a trance. His voice took on the voice of an old woman and muttered warnings to the young couple about danger to their bairn. They **must** take it to the hospital.

Next day the young tenants were told what had happened in their forsaken flat. They were sceptical, yet at the same time were cautiously admitting that they knew of an old woman who was related to them who had spoken in such a way. But she had been dead for some time.

Still, there was nothing wrong with their child. So, reluctantly and shamefacedly they made their way to the hospital — and were glad ever after that they had. For unbeknown to them the child had something stuck in its throat which could have caused its death.

The bathtub phantom of Blythswood Square

The folk who lived around Blythswod Square were sorry for the dark-haired foreign-looking young woman married to such a grumpy old man. Why, he was old enough to be her grandfather!

It must have been his wealth that made her parents agree to such a mis-matched alliance. And in those far off days young girls, especially foreigners, accepted the marriages arranged for them.

The beautiful young bride had a very dull time. Not for her the parties and outings she obviously longed for.

Her wistful eyes made the neighbours sympathetic — but all their friendly overtures were firmly repulsed by the crabbit old man who was her husband.

As the days and weeks went by however, it became apparent that the meek young bride had a volatile temper —the Spanish blood in her coming out no doubt, said the neighbours knowingly, as they heard the heated quarrels and screaming arguments between the couple.

Then one day the curtains remained closed. The doctor came. The undertaker came.

Word soon got round that the old man had collapsed and died in the bath in one of the fainting fits to which he was prone.

As soon as the funeral was over the young widow disappeared — back to a warmer climate, according to the local gossips.

The house stood empty for a while. Then along came a prospective buyer who was keen to live in that salubrious area.

He liked the house and its surroundings. It seemed just the thing for his wife and family, with enough accommodation for their servants too. It would need decorating of course, especially the bathroom which was grimly old fashioned.

But the buyer felt uneasy. There was something almost sinister in its atmosphere.

He decided against buying it; he would look for something else in the same neighbourhood.

His wife was furious. She was all in favour of the house. It was just what she wanted. The price was right. Why didn't he clinch the deal?

She stared in disbelief when he said he didn't like the bathroom! He'd felt frightened in it!

Away from the house his fears seemed irrational, especially with the scornful nagging of his beloved wife.

He bought the house. It was all decorated and the bathroom modernised. At last came the day when the family and servants could move in.

The head of the household went upstairs to view his modernised bathroom. He still felt uneasy. He wasn't going to have a bath in that place! He refused to go in unless he could leave the door open.

His wife, the children and the servants were all very happy

in their new home. They had no complaints about the bathroom.

The woman had reason for complaint though when he didn't have a bath for weeks. At last he nervously decided he would have to be brave. He was the head of the household, after all!

So, one night, when all the others had retired to bed, he left the bedroom carrying two candles. He ran the bath. Lovely hot water filled up the gleaming new white bath he had had installed. How silly he was, he convinced himself, as he shut the bathroom door.

He disrobed and made his way towards the bath. He heard a rustling noise. Quickly he turned to see what it was. It came from the direction of the grate. But there was nothing there.

He turned again towards the bath. Again there was a rustling noise. And again there was nothing in the grate.

He turned to get his ablutions over as quickly as possible and tripped. The candles went out. He was in darkness, and he could hear strange noises.

He lay petrified. The rustling grew nearer. He felt someone stepping on him!

It was a woman and he could feel the hems of her clothing. From the bath came the sounds of someone splashing as they luxuriated in the hot water.

Suddenly the splashing noises changed. They grew more frenzied, almost as if someone were struggling. Then all was quiet.

In the darkness the terrified man lay trembling. Again he could hear stealthy steps retreating towards the cupboard. Then suddenly he could see a face glowing. It was a strangely beautiful face but one contorted with hatred.

As soon as the apparition disappeared into the cupboard the man on the floor felt the atmosphere lighten slightly. He picked himself up and ran back to the bedroom.

He couldn't convince his wife that he had had such a terrifying experience. For the next few days the household continued happily in its daily pursuits, with the head of the house still un-bathed.

Then one morning came screams of terror as his eldest son entered the bathroom. Mother, servants, brothers and sisters all ran to the rescue.

Father remained where he was. He knew what was wrong.

The boy jabbered about an old man floating in the bath. Yet it was empty, gleaming white as usual.

His mother was cross. He must have been eavesdropping on her conversations with his father. The rescue contingent turned to leave the bathroom.

As they came out of the door and made their way to the stairs a woman silently passed them and disappeared into the cupboard through the closed door!

The servants grew hysterical A shaken wife at last acknowledged that her husband wasn't suffering from an over-fertile imagination after all.

The family vacated the house as soon as they could. It was then they learned about the previous owner who had 'died' in his bath.

It is anyone's guess as to whether the old man's death was due to 'natural causes'!

Singing ghost on the Glasgow Underground!

Some of Glasgow's ghosts choose the most mundane places to haunt — like the Underground!

Why should a beautiful lady in evening dress take a lonely walk along the platform at Hillhead station in the early hours of the morning? No one knows who she is or where she goes.

She certainly isn't making her solitary way home depressed at her escort's desertion, for she sings happily at the top of her voice, serenading the few Underground workers who are tidying up. Then she suddenly disappears into one of the dark tunnels.

The few who have heard her marvel at her beautiful voice and stand quietly until she passes, fearful that any untoward movement on their part may interrupt the rendering that holds them enthralled.

Another ghost prefers to visit a clothiers shop near the town centre. This ghost too is not fearsome, for he is a pleasant old-fashioned man, content to sit on a chair and watch all the comings and goings.

As long as people ignore him he is happy, but shyness overcomes him if anyone approaches him and he quickly disappears.

With all the life and death drama that occurs daily in hospital life it is little wonder that such places are said to be haunted.

Glasgow's Western Infirmary is no exception. This time, though, the ghost has been very firmly identified — and the circumstances leading up to its taking its abode there are well known.

At the turn of the century one of the leading surgeons in Glasgow was Sir William MacEwen. He specialised in brain surgery, but as the years went past he felt his hands beginning to shake after a short time and his work load had to be curtailed.

He carried on, of course, as long as he was able, for his skill in the operating theatre made him the most sought after surgeon in his field. At the age of seventy six he was still operating, albeit fewer and fewer people were benefiting from his expertise.

One day a young man, an artist, came into the hospital. He was suffering dreadfully from headaches.

Sir William refused to operate. He had done enough for that day and he felt it wouldn't be safe to take on another tricky operation without a good night's rest. The young man would be better to come back another day.

But as the young man left, agonising pain struck yet again. He couldn't see where he was going, so great was his distress. He stumbled and fell down the stairs.

When horrified staff rushed to help it was too late. He was dead.

Sir William never recovered from his shock at the outcome of his refusal to operate that day. The surgeon who had spent his life in easing the distress of so many was haunted by that tragic accident.

He died shortly after — and to this day his ghost can be seen haunting the corridor and stairs where the talented young artist's life ended so suddenly.

Bewitched! Invisible forces terrorise girl

There wasn't much by way of entertainment laid on for ordinary folk in the last decade of the 17th century, so when word got around of the thrilling spectacle to be seen at the McGilchrist residence in the Trongate, people flocked from far and near to see the ten-year-old girl reputed to be under the spell of witchcraft.

One minute she would be an ordinary youngster taking a youthful interest in all around her in the big 'toon' to which she had been brought in search of a cure, the next, she would be having a fit, performing all sorts of weird contortions and spilling from her mouth all sorts of rubbish — lumps of hair, pins, coal, bones ..... anything at all seemed to flood out of her mouth in such great quantity it was a wonder she didn't choke.

Then after all the screaming, moaning and yelling was over, and she returned to normal, she would tell of people who were tormenting her during her ordeal.

It all began in August 1696. Christian Shaw was the eldest daughter in a family of six. Her father, the well-respected John Shaw, Laird of Bargarran, near Erskine, had married one of the McGilchrists, a wealthy merchant family of Glasgow, and they were well enough off to have several servants living in.

It was one of these servants, a young girl from the Highlands, Katherine Campbell by name, who was accused of being responsible for all the trials and tribulations of the Shaw family over the next few months.

She had a quick temper, and when young Christian 'clyped' to her mother that she had seen Katherine Campbell steal a drink of milk, the servant lass waited until her mistress had taken herself off after roundly scolding her, then she got hold of young Christian and cursed her.

The other servants were horrified but it soon passed from their minds. Then a week later, Christian began to have some very weird experiences.

She seemed to go into a trance in which she was terribly troubled and in great pain. When this persisted for two or three days a doctor was summoned — but could find no explanation.

Days of normality were succeeded in turn by days when the youngster was in agony, calling out sometimes that she couldn't see. She had violent spasms, then went rigid and dumb, but always seemed to be in torment from unseen forces that only she could identify.

The house always seemed to be full of people wanting to see for themselves the strange happenings — and all were willing to testify that, in their opinion, the maid was bewitched.

The minister arranged to hold a weekly prayer meeting in the home, but still Christian continued to have the weird fits.

The doctor declared himself baffled — and advised that the child be taken to Glasgow for a specialist opinion.

Word was sent to Mrs Shaw's brother and he eagerly agreed that his niece and her father should stay with him in his house in the Trongate. They sailed from Erskine — and Christian enjoyed the journey in excellent health. Only once did she have an attack while they were in Glasgow.

Back home again all was well — until a fortnight later when their tribulations started over again.

Only now would her parents put into words the dreaded thought that had never been far from their minds, and they acknowledged that maybe the opinion so readily given by neighbours and friends could be true — Christian was be-witched.

Back in Glasgow again the attacks occurred with unfailing regularity — and word spread, so folk flocked to the Trongate to see the cursed maiden. And all were agog to hear the names that tripped off her tongue as being the ones who were the cause of all her torment.

Chief among them, of course, was Katherine Campbell, along with several other names of people who lived around Bargarran. And it was noticed that at the forefront of the mixed crowd in the Trongate were certain persons from 'outside' the town — and they seemed to be taking a particular delight in all the happenings.

The Glaswegian authorities became alarmed. It was all very well for a day or two to have such 'entertainment' — but if the lassie was indeed bewitched, and it seemed to have been going on for weeks with no cure, maybe it would be as well to demand that she be sent home — after all, the evil influence might spread around the town.

Also, the furore was attracting an undesirable element into their district. 'Yes, Christian Shaw must go', they declared.

More and more Christian's talk while she was having these fits was implicating Katherine Campbell and the other women in evil practices.

The family returned home and matters seemed to grow worse as each day went by, until the local minister decided he would have to enlist the aid of the Privy Council in Edinburgh to have certain locals arrested for witchcraft.

Having heard all the details the Privy Council finally agreed to appoint a Commission to examine all the evidence.

In the meantime Christian grew more and more violent. Her father decided to take matters into his own hands. He would arrest and detain for questioning all those whose names Christian so consistently recited in her torment.

Katherine Campbell, who by this time had fled from the house, was apprehended and lodged in Paisley Prison.

The Commission appointed by the Privy Council met and began their investigations. Those arraigned before them as being in thrall to witchcraft covered all ages and stations in life, from vagrants and vagabonds to respectable women regarded as pillars of the Church They were charged with meeting in covens to worship and serve the devil and wreak his evil upon an innocent child who had offended one of them

Christian was present at the inquiry and one way of

Folk watch in horror as Christian is thrown about by invisible forces after pulling giant hairs from her mouth

determining their guilt was to order the accused to touch her, and as they did so one by one, those who were guilty caused her to have a violent fit. One of the younger women seemed prepared to turn 'King's evidence' to incriminate her erstwhile fellow servants of the devil.

For nearly a fortnight investigations went on. Finally it was decided that twenty four people were to be reported as being suspected of witchcraft.

While all this was going on Christian Shaw seemed to be suffering more and more torment. Strange markings appeared on her, as if she had been bitten again and again. 'The devil having his revenge', opined the knowing ones.

A few weeks later another Commission was set up — this time not just to inquire into the practice of witchcraft but to try the accused.

At the end of March Christian had a particularly hard time — all night she seemed to be fighting a battle. At times she despaired and cried out.

This time she vowed the devil himself was trying to take control of her, now that his servants were no longer free to do his evil work, but she kept affirming her belief in God who would guard her and keep her. The next morning she was confidently stating that her tribulations were over.

The trial of the accused witches began in mid-April. Twenty of the original twenty five were brought to court.

Various tests and physical examinations were set to determine whether the accused were truly witches.

Trial was adjourned for a week or two to allow more evidence to be gathered. During this period another two women decided to confess their sin and implicate some of their fellow-prisoners.

In mid-May it was felt that sufficient convincing evidence was held to bring seven of the accused to trial.

The evidence against three men and four women was heard and they were found guilty.

All seven were sentenced to die on the gallows, their bodies to be immediately burned. One of the condemned was Katherine Campbell.

Sentence was carried out on Paisley gallows on June 10 and made a 'must' day out for citizens from all surrounding towns and villages, a large contingent attending from Glasgow where the possessed bairn had provided such great entertainment.

Christian Shaw, the ten-year-old who had suffered months of torment and fits, from that day on was free of bewitchment and curse.

But Christian Shaw was to be remembered for more than her involvement in the trial and execution of witches. She lived quietly at home until, in her mid-thirties, she married John Miller, a clergyman

from Kilmaurs in Ayrshire, only to become widowed within two years.

Determined to live her own life and pursue her own interests she refused to settle permanently back in Bargarran.

She took a house in Johnstone, near Paisley, and experimented in spinning thread. Then, in partnership with a Glasgow businessman and using equipment from Holland, then the chief centre of thread-making, she established a business that was soon turning out a high quality product.

'Bargarran Thread' became famous. Business prospered and soon Paisley was enjoying the reputation of being world famous for its thread, the pioneer of its industry the woman who, as a young child, had had a curse put on her and had been the object of attention of witches.

Whipped through the streets by the hangman!

In the mid 18th century two brothers, both astute businessmen, made their fortunes in Glasgow.

It was the dearest wish of both Allan and Robert Dreghorn that their family should become one of the most prominent in the city, indeed in all Scotland. Both built themselves imposing mansions, and Allan's house in Clyde Street became quite a tourist attraction.

He was a bachelor however, so the brothers' hopes for the future glory of their family rested in Robert's only son, young Bob.

When Allan died young Bob inherited all his property and his money. After his own father died young Bob was one of the wealthiest men in Glasgow. Quite a catch for any young lady.

Alas, the brothers' ambitions came to naught, for Bob was so ugly that he was nicknamed 'Bob Dragon'. Not that that deterred him in any from courting as he really thought that he was every young girl's dream.

He became notorious for his pursuit of the fairer sex who regarded his every overture as a source of great amusement. Poor Bob was convinced in his own mind that the ladies hung on his every word and were extremely jealous of each other when he singled out any one for his attentions. Little did he realise just what a figure of fun he was.

Word got around in the community one day that Bob Dragon had been summoned to the Parish Kirk in Govan, there to be publicly rebuked on the stool of repentance for one of his many sins.

The kirk had never been so full as it was that Sunday. The crowds flocked to see this sight.

Instead of being ashamed at his 'punishment' Bob gloried in being the centre of attraction, especially when the minister congratulated him on his following.

'Oh! Mr Dreghorn, Mr Dreghorn, surely, surely, ye've been weel liked, for I have never seen a greater congregation all my days in this place: Yea, I am almost persuaded that every leddy in Glasgow is doon here the day to get a sight of you.'

The 'leddies' hung their heads and blushed — but Bob enjoyed himself immensely.

Poor Bob Dragon never did win one of the ladies he so ardently pursued, and so idiosyncratic did he become that he, one of the wealthiest men in Glasgow, imagined he was one of the poorest of the poor.

Airing his woes one day he was comforted when one of his listeners sarcastically promised that if the worst came to the worst he personally would see that Bob was admitted to the Poorhouse.

Bob begrudged every penny he had to spend, and so depressed did he become at his lack of success in winning a wife and at his 'poverty' that he comitted suicide.

His ghost haunted the mansion in Clyde Street for many a year. No one could be persuaded to buy or rent the property even for the nominal sum asked, so ugly was the ghost who haunted it.

At last, after several years, a gentleman who scorned such nonsense as 'haunted houses' bought the place.

A great house-warming party was held. The mansion was restored to life and Bob's ghost was not an uninvited guest.

But its new glory didn't last long. The daughter of the house was convinced it was haunted. Her father yielded to her pleas to leave and once again Bob Dragon's house stood empty.

Several years later George Provand bought the building to use as a paint factory, with the upper rooms to be used as his living-quarters. All went well — Bob Dragon's ghost was never seen.

Then in 1822 a group of late night revellers decided to peer in the window just to see if they could see the ghost. They didn't; but their eyes widened in horror at what they did see.

They hurried away and soon were gasping out to anyone they met about rivers of blood and the butchered bodies of two children they had seen.

Those who heard were in no doubt; Provand was in cahoots with the resurrectionists! And so now they knew what had become of the two little chimney-boys who had gone missing. The poor little souls were hacked to bits!

As the early hours of the morning gave way to daylight, and more and more people heard the dreadful news, so the crowd grew and the dreadful discovery of how Bob Drgaon's house was being used infuriated the good people of Glasgow. They marched to Clyde Street, yelling and screaming vengeance.

George Provand, bewildered, heard the noise of the mob as he lay in bed on that Sunday morning, and got up to see what all the noise was about.

He peered out of his window. A stone, quickly followed by others, clattered against the pane.

From the frenzied screams he at last made out what had caused the riot.

In vain he tried to point out that he was no resurrectionist. But the maddened crowd would not be convinced that the 'rivers of blood' seen by the inebriated men was only red paint! Nor that the 'two chimneysweep boys' were two black tins containing paint!

No one at all would listen as he desperately shouted down from his window. The rioting mob were intent on destruction — man and property.

Provand managed to escape out a small back window and make his way to safety while the mob were breaking down his front door and smashing their way in through his street-level windows.

They rampaged through the building, breaking furniture, upsetting paint everywhere, destroying anything and everything, all at fever pitch. And all this on the Sabbath day.

All poor Provand's belongings were carted down to the river and thrown in — except for valuable silver, which soon found its way to other homes.

The police tried to intervene to restore order and were routed. All morning the destruction went on, until the army was called in to quell the mob. It took a cavalry charge with drawn swords to scatter the mob. The Riot Act was read.

The police and magistrates were appalled at the havoc. Grimly they resolved to bring the ring-leaders to book.

A reward of 200 guineas was offered for information leading to the arrest of those most guilty.

Some, ashamed of the way they had been led, bitterly regretting all that had happened to an innocent man's property, and realising it was only by the grace of God that a poor lonely old soul hadn't been lynched, came forward with information.

A number of arrests were made. Four of the leading rioters were sentenced to fourteen years transportation.

Another, Richard Campbell, was deemed to be the worst offender of all as he was an ex-policeman. In fact he'd been the chief stirrer of the mob against the police!

He not only shared the fourteen years transportation sentence but he was publicly whipped through the streets of Glasgow. The very last man to be so punished in the city.

Starting off at the front of the jail, he was tied to a cart and dragged round the streets, surrounded by dragoon guards to help control the crowds who had come to see.

Four times the procession stopped, and at each stopping-place the hangman, who also served as the meter-out of such punishment, brought out his 'cat-o'-nine-tails' and lashed down on Campbell's bare back — 20 lashes at each stop!

Such was the awful result of an impetuous desire to see if Bob Dragon's ghost was still haunting his old home!

A hangman's rope for 'the human crocodile'!

Five children, the eldest thirteen, were left orphans when their father, Dr Edward William Pritchard, was hanged in Jail Square, opposite Glasgow Green, in 1865.

Doubly orphaned, for their father had poisoned their mother just a few months earlier.

And their granny too.

It was the last public execution in Glasgow, and in accordance with his life, it was turned into an 'occasion' by the victim, for even as he faced death by hanging, Dr Pritchard enjoyed playing to the crowd and being the centre of attraction.

In life he had been a tall well-groomed 'gentleman' who gloried in making his presence felt as he walked the streets.

In death he did not disappoint the crowds who had turned up to see him hang.

He insisted on wearing his best suit and white gloves —and even ordered a new pair of patent boots for the occasion!

But as more and more details of his wickedness came to light, so more and more of those who had been taken in by his charm realised just what a charlatan he had been.

Why, he had pretended such grief at his wife's funeral that he had called for the coffin to be opened one last time that he might kiss his beloved farewell!

And all unbeknown to the other sorrowing relatives who were so supportive of him, he had been responsible for her death.

Crocodile tears, people murmured later .... and dubbed him 'the human crocodile'.

In the six years he lived in Glasgow Dr Pritchard certainly made his mark. He became a well-known public figure in no time — he was always available to give lectures; he became a leading Freemason; he claimed medical qualifications far in excess of those he actually possessed; he was a 'character' who amused ordinary folk as they cheerfully accepted a photograph of himself handed out by the doctor in the streets; they half-believed his story that he was a personal friend of Garibaldi who was hitting the headlines in the world's press at the time ... But there were those, more sober medical men, who were very dubious about him. He was a braggart and a liar; yet his personality might have made him an entertaining one .... had he not turned to murder.

Edward William Pritchard was born in the South of England in 1825 and those of his family who did not follow a medical career took up a naval career.   Edward Pritchard combined both. On shore leave one day he was introduced to the daughter of a wealthy Edinburgh merchant — romance was quickly followed by marriage, and as Mary Jane pined for her husband while he was away at sea, her wealthy father bought Pritchard out of the Navy and installed him in a practice in Yorkshire. One thing that came to light after his trial was his reputation in Yorkshire of being a womaniser.

A few years after the family had settled in Yorkshire his in-laws bought him a practice in Glasgow and there they settled — well, not exactly 'settled', for in their six years in Glasgow they had three different homes.

Suspicion attached itself to Dr Pritchard as being responsible for a tragedy in their first Glasgow home. While his wife was away visiting her folks one night, a mysterious fire broke out in the servants' attic — and a young girl was burned to death. There were whispers that the maid was pregnant (with the doctor as father of course), and there were vague rumours of suspicious circumstances about how the fire started — but nothing could be proved, and a verdict of 'Death by Misadventure' was brought in at a subsequent inquiry.

A year later Pritchard's normally healthy wife began to suffer from vague illnesses. Again, it emerged later that the young fifteen-year old maid brought in to replace the one who had died in the fire had become the doctor's mistress.He is supposed to have promised her marriage, should his wife pre-decease him.

The vague illnesses turned into violent bouts of sickness. Only when she went home to her parents in Edinburgh to convalesce did she recover fully. Back home in Glasgow the sickness started up again, so Mary Jane's mother came to take charge of the household and nurse her daughter. Two weeks later she too was very ill. A local doctor named Paterson was called and he gave Pritchard no hope of his mother-in-law recovering. A day or two later the old lady died — and Dr Paterson refused to sign a death certificate. All this time Edward Pritchard had been purchasing deadly poisons.

Dr Paterson made several visits to Mary Jane over the next three weeks or so after her mother's death — and always her husband seemed to be distraught at her illness, and anxious to do anything to help her recover. But in the early hours of the morning of March 18, 1865, Mary Jane died an agonising death.

Expressions of sympathy poured in to the seemingly heartbroken widower. But the police moved swiftly when an anonymous 'tip-off' suggested there might be suspicious circumstances surrounding two such violent deaths. Pritchard was arrested on suspicion of murder. Yes, poison was found in his wife's body, so it was felt expedient to exhume the old lady's body as well. Again poison was found. Pritchard, avowing his innocence, was sent for trial to Edinburgh on July 3, 1865. Five days later the jury delivered their unanimous verdict — Guilty!

Pritchard shortly before his execution

Three weeks later Dr Edward William Pritchard was the last person to be hanged in public in Glasgow.

In these three weeks he made three separate 'confessions'. First he said both he and the fifteen-year old maid were guilty.

In the second 'confession' he pleaded guilty to committing adultery with the maid — but insisted he had not murdered his mother-in-law.

In his final confession he pleaded guilty to poisoning both his wife and mother-in-law, but absolved the maid of all blame. It turned out the old lady had seen him making love to the young girl — and therefore she had to be got rid of.

There was no mention of the other young lassie burned to death, so he went to his doom taking with him that secret: Was he a double murderer or a triple murderer?

Secret romance ends in murder

In April 1928, when 92-year old Lena Sheehy died in New York she took with her to her grave the answer to a mystery that remains unsolved to this day.

For Lena Sheehy is better known as 'Madeleine Smith', the twenty-one year old Glasgow girl who was accused of poisoning her lover, Pierre Emile l'Angelier.

The general concensus of opinion to-day seems to be that she was indeed guilty, but the jury before which she was tried in Edinburgh in 1857 couldn't make up its mind — so brought in that unsatisfactory Scottish verdict, 'Not Proven'.

In other words, on the one hand they thought it very probable that she did commit murder, but the prosecution had failed to convince them conclusively: and on the other hand the defence had failed to convince them conclusively that she was innocent!

The 'Not Proven' verdict meant Madeleine was free to leave court.

The events leading up to that sensational trial began just over two years earlier in the spring of 1855 when a young lady, recently returned home from boarding-school, found life in Glasgow a bit of a bore, and so, to help relieve the tedium of shopping, parties, assemblies and other 'lady-like' pursuits, indulged in a clandestine relationship with an impoverished romantic-looking young man, a foreigner, she had seen at a few dances.

He too was just as keen as Madeleine for the 'coincidental' meeting in Sauchiehall Street which both of them had contrived to arrange.

Other rendezvous followed, and Madeleine's young sister Bessie was thrilled to be part of such romantic assignations — until she learned that the handsome young 'beau' was interested only in her sister.

Then she 'clyped'!

Madeleine's father was furious, and forbade her to associate with Pierre L'Angelier again.

Why, he was only a poorly paid clerk at Huggins, the Bothwell Street seedsmen.

How dare he aspire to the hand of the daughter of a well-respected Glasgow architect.

And to court her in secret — just the sort of underhand behaviour one would expect from a foreigner!

Madeleine wrote to tell Pierre that their association must come to an end.

But Pierre was not to give up so great a prize easily.

More meetings were arranged, this time aided and abetted by an elderly spinster who had befriended Pierre.

Fresh ructions followed when Madeleine's father found out the association was still going strong.

Again Madeleine wrote to finish things.

She may have thought her Pierre a handsome-looking and exciting wooer, but his looks belied him.

He wrote (again clandestinely) to Madeleine reproaching her for deceiving him — and also for deceiving her father by not telling him how close she had become to Pierre.

He was so aggrieved and full of self-pity that Madeleine again made overtures to renew their association.

For over a year their association continued.

The Smith family had a holiday home 'doon the watter' at Rhu where they spent most of the summer.

Here Madeleine found another ally in one of the maids, Christine Haggart, who acted as a 'go-between' for the lovers.

Madeleine again found excitement and thrills in secret meetings and smuggling her lover into her bedroom — and lovers they were by this time.

In between all the secret meetings and rendezvous at various 'safe houses' Madeleine was a prolific letter-writer.

Her Pierre kept her letters — and after his death nearly two hundred were found!

In them Madeleine had frequently referred to Pierre as her 'husband'.

Some especially caused a sensation when they were read in court. ....'If we did wrong last night it was in the excitement of our love.' 'We should, I suppose, have waited till we were married.'

Pierre, on the other hand, was the one to express guilt! 'I am sad at what we did, I regret it very much.'

Then he goes on to blame Madeleine — and her parents! Everybody and anybody was to blame — but not Pierre!

'Why did you give way after your promises?'

'We did wrong. It is your parents' fault if shame is the result: they are to blame for it all.'

Still Madeleine continued to bombard her 'husband' with letters vowing her undying love.

A few months more passed until towards the end of '56 Pierre thought he could detect a 'cooling-off' in his beloved's epistles.

He began to hear tales of her association with another young man — an open association, welcomed by her family.

Then in January '57 came a devastating blow — Madeleine was engaged to someone else and she wanted her letters back. This time Pierre's despair and threats of revealing all to her family didn't bring his 'wife' back to him.

She pretended to be remorseful and desirous of a reconciliation but at the same time began to buy arsenic.

She told various chemists from whom she purchased it that the poison was needed to get rid of rats.

Again there were more secret meetings with Pierre, when she plied him with cups of cocoa to keep out the cold as he hung around outside her bedroom window at the Smith house in Blythswood Square to which the family had recently moved.

Every time he returned home from one of these trysts he was extremely ill — but wouldn't believe it could be any of his beloved's doing.

Madeleine by now was courting her 'official' fiance in earnest; the wedding was planned .... and she was still desperately trying to keep things smooth with Pierre.

On March 23, 1857, in the early hours of the morning Pierre L'Angelier died an agonising death.

Suicide was rumoured — but soon discounted.

From various interviews Madeleine soon realised that suspicion was falling on her.

She fled to Rhu — but was persuaded to return to Glasgow by her fiance.

She was arrested on March 31, 1857.

The trial was held in Edinburgh.

Madeleine was cool, calm and collected.

The defence portrayed Pierre L'Angelier as an impoverished adventurer, out to make an advantageous marriage; a man who was pretentious and conceited, yet easily thrown into melancholy and despair when life was not going his way.

Witnesses were produced from his earlier life who testified that he had on occasions threatened suicide.

The prosecution had plenty of damning letters which showed Madeleine as being infatuated and committed, then desperately trying to end the association when her fancy turned in another direction — but there were no witnesses to a meeting having actually taken place betweeen the two erstwhile lovers within the last few days of L'Angelier's life.

Madeleine maintained she had not seen him for about

three weeks before his death, and yes, she had written and begged him to visit her that she might explain and reason with him, but he had ignored her pleas.

Nine days after the trial began the verdict was given — 'Not Proven'.

But what happened to the 21-year old Madeleine Smith in the intervening years before her death as 92-year old Lena Sheehy?

Her parents were devastated by the events and the trial — so much so that neither of them was able to attend it to support her.

Her fiance deserted her as soon as the verdict was given.

It was felt expedient for Madeleine to make herself scarce for a while.

Four years later in 1861 Madeleine Smith married George Wardle whom she had met in Plymouth in the home of an acquaintance who had taken her in.

They settled in London, had a son and daughter, and became leading lights in the district in which they lived.

For twenty-eight years married life suited Madeleine well — then George deserted her.

For the next few years her movements were uncertain.

Then at the age of 80 she went to live in America with her son, met and married Sheehy, and settled in New York. She lived out the rest of her life quietly and died in 1928, two years after being widowed.

To this day opinion is divided as to whether or not she did indeed murder her lover Pierre L'Angelier by poison.

A cup of cocoa for her lover — but had she poisoned it?

Innocent! but he spent 18 years in jail for a murder he didn't commit

On Thursday May 6, 1909, Oscar Slater was found guilty of murder and sentenced to death. He was to be hanged on Thursday May 27.

On February 3, 1948, Oscar Slater died peacefully at his home in Ayr, aged 75.

In the intervening years he had spent over eighteen years in Peterhead Prison for a crime of which he was innocent.

The murder of which he was accused and found guilty took place a day or two before Christmas, 1908.

An 83-year-old wealthy spinster was battered to death in her flat in West Princes Street, Glasgow.

Her maid, Helen Lambie, had been out of the house only ten minutes to fetch a newspaper for her mistress. When she returned she found an agitated neighbour on the doorstep, worried at all the banging and bumping that had been coming from the normally quiet flat upstairs.

Together they went to investigate — and as they entered the flat a man in a fawn overcoat rushed out.

Strangely enough Helen Lambie was not perturbed when she saw him. But a minute later she was screaming for the neighbour, Arthur Adams, to come quickly.

In the blood-spattered dining-room lay the battered body of her mistress.

Immediately Arthur Adams thought of the man who had left as they entered, and ran down to the street — but not a soul was to be seen.

A doctor and the police were summoned and given the facts. Helen Lambie was asked to look and see if anything was missing.

Amongst the debris lay an opened wooden box, and round it were scattered items of jewellery. Only a diamond brooch was missing, as far as she could tell, said Helen.

Next she gave a description of the man seen leaving the

They find the battered body

flat. It was a description Arthur Adams could only vaguely confirm as he was not wearing his glasses.

When the horrific crime was reported in the newspapers a 14-year-old girl came forward to say she had seen a man in a fawn overcoat racing along the street about that time, but her description did not tally.

The police came in for a lot of criticism when they failed to solve the murder, so when a cycle-dealer came forward with information about a foreigner who lived locally and who had been trying to sell a pawn ticket for a diamond brooch, they were jubilant.

They swooped on the address — only to find their quarry had sailed for America!

Their suspicions of him grew when investigations revealed that Oscar Slater had several aliases. He seemed a shady character ; he frequented sleazy gaming-clubs; he co-habited with a prostitute — just the sort of character who would be capable of murder, concluded the police.

And as he had fled the country this only went to prove he was fleeing from justice. They cabled their counterparts in New York to arrest Slater on his arrival aboard the 'Lusitania'.

By the time Slater was arrested in New York the police in Britain had investigated further and found that his passage had been booked weeks before the murder and that the diamond brooch had been pawned weeks before as well and was certainly **not** the one stolen from the murdered lady's flat.

Nevertheless the police proceeded with their endeavours to pin the murder on their only suspect.

The three witnesses were given a free trip to America to identify Slater — which they did, albeit uncertainly.

Extradition was arranged. Slater made no demur — after all, he was innocent, he protested, so he was quite willing to return to Glasgow in order that the misunderstanding and false accusations could be cleared up. On his arrival he was taken to Edinburgh for trial.

On Monday May 3, 1909, the trial began.

The prosecution was very convincing: the defence did its best, but the judge, an intensely religious man, was biased against the prisoner — a gambler, a womaniser, a foreigner, a shady character. This was just the very sort of man who would murder a defenceless old lady, he opined.

Slater was found guilty and led away, still protesting his innocence, to suffer three weeks of mental torture while he awaited his rendezvous with the hangman.

But the public, who had been jubilant at an arrest, had followed the trial eagerly. At the end, when sentence was passed, quite a number of people felt uneasy. They were not so convinced as they had been that the true murderer had been caught.

Some felt so strongly that there had been a miscarriage of justice that they got up a petition. More than 20,000 people signed, asking for a reprieve.

Several well-known personalities took an interest in the case and championed Slater, among them Arthur Conan Doyle and Andrew Lang.

So great was the pressure that, only two days before the hanging, the Scottish Secretary announced a reprieve had been granted .... but Slater was to be committed to Peterhead Prison.

In the next year or two some of his supporters campaigned on his behalf and in 1914 a secret inquiry was held, but again the verdict was against Slater.

Then the First World War broke out and the Slater affair became less important to his supporters. By the end of the war Slater had been forgotten.

Several years went by and then one evening in 1925 Sir Arthur Conan Doyle had a visitor — an old lag recently released from Peterhead Prison. He brought with him a desperate plea from Slater for Sir Arthur to once again take up his case.

Conan Doyle was perturbed that he had allowed a case in which he had so fervently believed to be shoved to the back of his mind. Again he agitated on Slater's behalf and the affair once again began to fill many columns of newsprint.

The authorities were under great pressure to act. In mid-November, 1927, Oscar Slater was released from prison.

Then he and his supporters were not satisfied merely with his freedom. They demanded an inquiry. Slater still avowed his innocence.

Again publicity and pressure from well-known figures won the day. An inquiry was held in June 1928 — and this time it was agreed that an appeal would be heard in July.

When the results of the appeal were announced it seemed at first as though it was to be frustration and disappointment again for Slater.

Then in the final sentences of his address the Lord Justice General stated that the jury had been mis-directed in the original trial and therefore the conviction would be set aside.

Slater decided that was as much as he could hope for and made up his mind to press no further for a declaration of his innocence. He was later awarded £6,000 compensation for his nineteen years wrongful imprisonment.

Satan's witches torment St Patrick

One verse of 'The Song of the Clyde' starts off:

'There's Pa and Ma doon at the Broomiela'
They're ga'en doon the watter for the Fair .....'

To Glasgwegians of old 'doon the watter' (The Clyde) was **the** place for a holiday, even if it was just one day.

Steamers and trains filled up with eager crowds, transporting them to various resorts on the Clyde like Gourock, Dunoon, Largs and Rothesay, which all offered joys untold to Glaswegians.

And for those who preferred more solitude and quietness there were Wemyss Bay and Innellan, Kilcreggan and Cove — with many another delightful resort if you ventured up one of the 'lochs' which fed the Clyde, or even sailed up the Kyles of Bute to a village delighting in the name of 'Tighnabruaich'.

For those who decided to sail down the Clyde on their holiday, after the 'industrial' river was left behind, there was plenty to interest the seeker after tales and legends.

From the centre of Glasgow to Erskine at one time there were no fewer than eleven ferry crossings with the Erskine Ferry the last before the 'holiday' Clyde was reached. Now a road bridge carries the traffic across the river from Erskine to Old Kilpatrick.

Local folk claim that St Patrick, patron saint of Ireland, was born here. (A claim also made by a place in Wales!)

He so infuriated the devil with his piety that Satan ordered an army of witches to torment the staunch Christian. Patrick decided to flee, and sailed off down the Clyde, for witches have no power over running water.

The devil was even more furious when he saw his minions being frustrated. He clawed out a boulder from the nearby hillside and heaved it at the fleeing saint. Fortunately he missed.

The Devil hurls a rock as St Patrick sails away

But the rock is still there in the Clyde for all to see — the huge rock known as 'Dumbarton Rock'. (Although, as with all good legends, there are variations, and a claim is made for a much smaller rock, St Patrick's Stone, near Old Kilpatrick.)

On Dumbarton Rock itself stands an old castle, now a museum, featured in many a tale of Scotland's past heroes and heroines.

The Rock was valued as a natural fortress by the Romans and the Ancient Britons, and 'Dumbarton' is said to take its name from 'Dun Breattan' — the Fortress of the Britons.

It became a royal stronghold in the Middle Ages and one of its governors, in the days of Wallace, was Sir John Menteith, who captured the Scottish leader and handed him over to the enemy.

In 'Tales of a Grandfather' Sir Walter Scott recounts the story of Wallace's betrayal — said to have been at Robroyston, when Wallace was having a meal with a party of supposed friends.

Menteith had arranged a signal — when he turned over a loaf of bread on the table, that was the signal for his men to pounce on the unsuspecting Wallace and take him prisoner.

From there, so legend says, Scotland's hero was taken to Dumbarton, there to await his transportation to England and trial in London. And, says Scott, from that day it was not considered good form to turn over a loaf of bread in the presence of anyone named Menteith, as it reminded them of the treachery of their forebear!

Another legend says Scotland's only 'lake', Lake of Menteith, near the Trossachs, is called 'lake' instead of 'loch' because 'Fause Menteith' betrayed Wallace!

Visitors can see images of Wallace and Menteith, one on each side of an entrance at the castle. Which is which? The one standing with his finger in his cheek is Menteith — the 'give away' sign of a traitor.

Another prisoner here at one time, according to official history, was the infamous 'Bad Lord Soulis' of Hermitage Castle.

He died in Dumbarton Castle, imprisoned for insurrection against Robert the Bruce ..... which is not so exciting a story as the legend that says that when Bruce was weary of so many complaints against the evil earl he said 'Hang him, boil him, do anything you

Rolled in a sheet of lead and plunged into the cauldron

like with him, but let me hear no more of him' ..... and the complainants took him literally! They did just as he suggested!

:They rolled him in a sheet of lead
A sheet of lead for a funeral pall.
They plunged him in a cauldron red,
And melted him, lead, bones and all!'

Many other exciting escapades took place in Dumbarton Castle — it was captured and recaptured on numerous occasions.

Further down the Clyde on the opposite bank to Dumbarton is Port Glasgow, the town especially developed from the small fishing village of Newark in the late 17th century to serve as a 'port' for Glasgow when that city was rapidly developing its trade, and none of the existing ports on the Clyde were very much in favour of more trade coming into their harbours to find its way up to the 'big toon'. So Glasgow got its own back on them by building its own 'Port Glasgow'.

Then about a century later some expert proposed a means of deepening the Clyde making the city accessible to big ships and Port Glasgow's heyday was over!

Next door to Port Glasgow is Greenock, where devotees of Burns will no doubt be keen to pay their respects at the grave of 'Highland Mary' — the lassie from Dunoon, across the Clyde, to whom Burns plighted his troth over a burn, each holding a Bible in their hand. (At the same time he was supposedly 'engaged' to another.)

Burns and Highland Mary planned to go to the West Indies, and Mary set off for home to break the news to her family that she was going to emigrate.

Mary came back to Greenock to rendezvous with her beloved, but while staying with relatives in Charles Street, caught a fever and died.

'Highland Mary' features in a few of Burns' poems — 'Will Ye Go to the Indies, My Mary?': 'To Mary in Heaven': and of course, 'Highland Mary'.

Why the sailors were superstitious about Granny Kempock

Greenock and the 'Port' are industrial areas, Gourock is the residential resort. Gourock was known as a port as far back as the late 15th century when King James IV decided it was the place to set out from on an expedition to quieten the Western Isles.

Perhaps the sailors who manned his ships visited 'Granny Kempock' before setting off.

'Granny Kempock' is a 6ft high grey stone monolith with extraordinary powers — or so thought fishermen and sailors in days of old. Visiting 'Granny Kempock' to walk seven times round her, scattering sand from the nearby shore, ensured a good catch and no rough seas for local fishermen.

Sailors who were venturing further afield made sure they carried aboard their ship some soil dug up from around Granny's base — then they would be sure to have a safe voyage and a happy return to their home port.

Imagine the rage, mingled with fear, then, when it became known in 1662 that a local lass, Mary Lamont, long suspected of being a witch, confessed that she and fellow-members of her coven had actually plotted to take 'Granny' and throw her in the Clyde! Then instead of bringing good luck, she would cause endless shipwrecks!

Mary was only 18 but she and her fellow-conspirators were burned at the stake for this alleged plan! Granny Kempock remains to this day.

The Cloch Lighthouse on the shore betweeen Gourock and Inverkip is a well-known landmark that features on many a postcard.

Inverkip is a small village, quieter now that traffic no longer thunders through since the by-pass was built, but for a small village it had more than its share of less than law-abiding inhabitants. In the 17th century it was the centre which all witches and warlocks from the surrounding area looked on as their 'headquarters'. Then, when witchcraft died out, in the 18th century and early 19th century the locals got their thrills from smuggling!

One of the local gentry, Alexander Lindsay of Dunrod, was the leading warlock of the district.

'Auld Dunrod was a goustie carle (ghostly looking fellow)
As ever ye micht see:
And gin he wasna a warlock wicht,
There was nane in the hale countrie.'

He got his just deserts, however, for his evil practices led to him losing the family estate and dying a pauper, beholden to one of his old tenants for a crust of bread and a bed in the barn.

By now of course, we are well out of the 'River' Clyde and in to the 'Firth' of Clyde, and across the Firth from Gourock is Holy Loch, well known now the world o'er as the base for American submarines.

A storm blows up and soil brought from
the Holy Land blows overboard

Locals will tell you that when Glasgow Cathedral was planned, the Bishop commissioned one of his men to fetch some earth from the Holy Land. This earth would be scattered beneath the foundations of the new Cathedral.

Alas, as the ship began sailing back up the Clyde a storm arose, it sank, and the precious cargo sank too. So, as beneath the loch lies soil from the Holy Land, what better name could be given to that stretch of water than 'Holy Loch'?

The land across the Firth from Gourock is indented with 'fiords' — Gare Loch, on which stands Rhu; Loch Long, with its own 'diversion' into Loch Goil; and Holy Loch, each with its cluster of resorts beloved by Glaswegians for their 'Fair'.

Across from Inverkip is Innellan where George Matheson lived as the parish minister for eighteen years.

Born in Glasgow, his eyesight had always been troublesome, and by the time he graduated from Glasgow University at the age of 19 he was totally blind. After two years as an assistant at a Glasgow church he came to Innellan as the parish minister.

Here he composed a hymn, as he himself says, 'My hymn was composed in the manse of Innellan on the evening of June 6, 1882. I was alone at the time. It was the day of my sister's marriage, and the rest of the family were staying overnight in Glasgow.

'Something had happened to me which was known only to myself, and which caused me the most severe mental suffering. The hymn was the fruit of that suffering.'

The hymn composed that night is sung at many a wedding — 'O Love that wilt not let me go'.

He doesn't say what had caused such great mental suffering — but the story has long persisted that he had been jilted because the young lady felt she couldn't spend the rest of her life with a blind man.

Bitter feud then 36 Lamonts hanged on a tree

This area, known as the Cowal Coast, had been Lamont territory for nearly 200 years, so they didn't take it very well when, towards the end of the 14th century, Robert the Bruce's grandson made a Campbell keeper of Dunoon Castle.

The Lamonts had never been supporters of the Bruces anyway, but now the Campbells too became their sworn enemies, and for nearly 300 years the feud smouldered. Mostly the Campbells had the upper hand, but in the years following the 'Solemn League and Covenant' the Lamonts, seizing a chance to settle old scores, sided with Montrose, and set off to harry the Campbells.

But again the Campbells proved too strong, and the Lamonts were besieged in Toward Castle. It seemed to be a stalemate, for the Lamonts were firmly ensconced in their stronghold.

The Campbells proposed an armistice, promising to spare the Lamonts if they would but yield. The Lamonts agreed.

But when they cautiously ventured out they were seized and carted off as prisoners to Dunoon Castle.

There 'not any of the name of Lamont that were passed seven years of age' was spared. Thirty-six prominent Lamonts were hanged on one tree — the rest were disposed of by other means!

Hardly a stone remains of Dunoon Castle now, and Toward Castle too is a ruin, not to be confused with Castle Toward, a mansion visible from steamers sailing into Rothesay Bay.

Perhaps of all the resorts 'doon the watter' Rothesay is the one most loved by Glaswegians. As our 'Song of the Clyde' says,

'And Scotland's Madeira, that's Rothesay, they say'.
Rothesay's ruined castle is right in the middle of the town whose history dates back to Viking times. The resident ghost is Lady Isobel, who is sometimes seen on the stairway known as 'the Bluidy Stair'.

A shriek is heard on the 'bluidy stair'

Her father and brothers were killed in a Viking raid — then their murderer had the audacity to propose marriage to the Lady Isobel! Rather than ally herself with her family's enemy she stabbed herself to death on the stairway.

'And aft in the mirk and midnicht hour,
When a' is silent there:
A shriek is heard, and a lady is seen,
On the steps o' the Bluidy Stair.'

Across on the south side of the Clyde again is Largs, another loved resort. Just behind the town is Brisbane Glen, home of the Brisbane family for over 600 years.

One of its sons, Sir Thomas Brisbane, was appointed Governor of New South Wales in Australia and in 1824 he selected the site for a new penal settlement. Nearly twenty years later the settlement was opened to free settlers as well, and in 1859 'Brisbane' became the capital of the colony of Queensland.

In Brisbane Glen is the grave of the Rev William Smith, minister at one of the churches in Largs. When the plague struck in 1644 he invited all those who suffered to isolate themselves in the glen, and he went with them to minister to them.

He himself caught the plague, and his grave, known as 'the prophet's grave', can still be seen. An iron gate leads into a pathway through a field to where he was buried.

Silent march of the legless legionaries!

When H V Morton was travelling in Scotland in the late 1920s gathering material for his book 'In Search of Scotland', an old Glaswegian told him, 'If you havna seen the Clyde you havna seen Glasgow.'

The industrial Clyde is famous. As many an old Glaswegian boasts, 'Glasgow made the Clyde, and the Clyde made Glasgow.'

But the Clyde runs for nearly 100 miles before it even reaches Glasgow!

The mighty river that brought prosperity and industry to St Mungo's 'dear green place' has to start somewhere! And that somewhere is nearly 100 miles up in the Lowther Hills.

As 'The Song of the Clyde' says:
'I sing of a river I'm happy beside
The song that I sing is the song of the Clyde;
Of all Scottish rivers it's dearest to me,
It flows from Leadhills, all the way to the sea.'

And as it 'flows from Leadhills' it passes through some lovely country, with almost forgotten little villages along its banks, many with an interesting tale to tell.

There isn't **one** spot to which you can go and say 'Here is the source of the Clyde' — for there are two or three claimants! Two or three little springs and trickles of burns start around here before meeting up to become 'the Clyde', so it just depends on which little village you visit which 'source of the Clyde' will be pointed out to you!

But as our song says 'Leadhills' we may as well start at the village of that name. It claims (at 1500 ft) to be the highest village in Scotland, but its near neighbour, Wanlockhead, also makes that claim!

'Leadhills' suggests that the mineral was mined here, as indeed it was — along with silver and gold, so much so that the area was nicknamed 'God's treasure house in Scotland'. It is still worthwhile to pan for gold in the streams — and when that pastime palls there is ski-ing in winter — and golf, where the golfer can then boast of having played on Britain's highest course!

Gold from this area was used when the Scottish crown, now in Edinburgh Castle, was refashioned in the days of James V.

Crawford, just a few miles away, looks a sleepy little village now, but in days of yore it was one of the stopping-places for coaches on the main road south.

Even further back, in Roman times, it was a strategic centre for the occupying forces, and from Crawford they sallied out to tackle the pockets of resistance fighters.

Local folk will tell you that a company of legless Legionaries

Legless legionaries on the march

are on occasion seen marching down the village en route to their endless task! (They are 'legless' because the road down which they march has been so built up since Roman times that it is quite a few inches higher than in bygone days ..... and the Roman soldiers are still marching on their own road!)

Crawford Castle was an ancient seat of the Lindsays, who, when ennobled took 'Crawford' as the title of their Earldom.

At one time the castle was used as a hunting-seat by James V, who brought a party of Frenchmen here for the hunt. They complained at the barrenness and bleakness of the surrounding countryside. It had no vegetation, they griped.

James promised them that that night at dinner they would have as their dessert a Scottish dish from that area that was richer by far than anything ever served up in France.

In solemnly marched the servants bearing for each guest a covered plate. The covers were removed, and to each man's astonishment before him lay a plate of gold and silver coins. 'The fruit of the district', the King told them drily.

For those who revel in gruesome tales a walk, in the nearby woods is a must! Count the number of trees on which a silver cross can be seen — then ask a villager what it all means.

'Och, you've been to the Hanging Wood', you'll be told. 'On every tree with a cross someone was hanged. Thieves, murderers ..... oh aye, and Jacobites!'

Gold and silver coins on every plate

Wife and servants burned to death

If Crawford proves too gruesome a place for you, hurry on to Lamington.

Tradition says that Marion Bradfute, wife of William Wallace, the great Scottish patriot, was born here.

Wallace had been involved in one or two minor skirmishes against the English from his youth, but it was as a reprisal against one of these skirmishes that Hazelrigg, the Governor of Lanark, set fire to Wallace's house, burning his wife Marion and her servants to death.

Local legend says that Hazelrigg had wanted the heiress Marion as a bride for his own son, and was enraged when she rejected him and chose the local youth who was a thorn in the side of the English troops, so he was glad of an excuse to wreak vengeance. But his revenge turned sour on him when Wallace from that time forth devoted all his energies to fighting the English and their minions successfully.

A few villages and towns around this area have their legends.

Wallace's home is set ablaze

Symington is the gathering place for those intent on climbing Tinto Hill.

Climbers who reach the top of the 2,335 ft rise are rewarded with a magnificent view stretching as far as Ireland on a clear day, to the Lake District, Arran in the Firth of Clyde and the Bass Rock off the east coast.

The problem for many though is whether to go when it is clear and enjoy the view, or to go when the top of the hill is shrouded in mist, in the hope of finding the hidden chest that contains the magic cup, which, when used to drink from, grants you your heart's desire.

'On Tintock Tap there is a mist,
And in the mist there is a kist,
And in the kist there is a caup,
And in the caup there is a draup.
Take up the caup; drink off the draup,
And set the caup on Tintock Tap.'

On Tinto Hill are the fragmentary remains of Fatlips Castle, said to have been at one time the home of one of the Symington lairds.

If you think its name peculiar, there is another Fatlips Castle on the summit of Mount Minto ..... one on Minto and one on Tinto!

The Minto Fatlips takes its name from a peculiarity of the notorious Border freebooter, Turnbull of Barnhill, who owned it, so it may well be that one of the Symington lairds was likewise blessed!

Further down the Clyde valley, at Carnwarth, is all that remains of Couthally Castle, sometimes spelt Cowthally Castle, once seat of the Somervilles.

Here they entertained royalty, and one local legend (accounting for the alternative spelling of its name) says the Somervilles were never short of visitors, so much so that they had to kill a cow each day of the year to cater for their guests' needs ..... so their castle became known as the 'Cow-daily' Castle!

Another story of the castle is one similar to a tale connected with two or three other castles in Scotland.

The castle was captured by the first Somerville, and as he had made quite a job of attacking it, it was uninhabitable when finally he was victorious. He decided to build a new castle on a more favourable site nearby — but every morning the workmen found their work of the previous day demolished.

They were getting nowhere fast, so Somerville, suspecting sabotage by supporters of the defeated foe, decided to keep watch one night and catch them at their evil work ..... but it was no human hand that was causing all the setbacks, for Somerville recognised the devil and his cohorts gleefully knocking down the walls built so painstakingly that day! And as they went about their destruction they warned:

"Tween the Rae Hill and Lorisburnshaw
There ye'll find Couthally wa'
And the foundations laid on iron.'

Somerville decided to take the hint, and the castle was rebuilt on the site of the original. Needless to say there were no more delaying tactics!

The Devil and his helpers were knocking down the castle
as fast as Somerville could build it

Saracen wife swaps magic jewel for captured husband

The Lockharts of Carnwarth are the guardians of the Lee Penny, an heirloom dating from the 14th century when Sir Simon Lockard accompanied the Good Sir James Douglas and his escort to the Holy Land, carrying with them the heart of Robert the Bruce, who had always longed to go on a crusade there, but was kept constantly on the alert for the defence of his realm, and dared not leave it lest the English take advantage of his absence to renew their efforts to conquer and rule Scotland. When Bruce was dying he charged his good friend Douglas to bury his heart in the Holy Land.

Alas, his wishes were never fulfilled, for the party allowed themselves to be diverted and become embroiled in warfare against the Saracens in Spain — a battle that was to end in the death of most of the party, Good Sir James included.

Sir Simon Lockard was one of the few survivors and he rescued his king's heart and, sadly, returned with it to Scotland.

In one of the skirmishes in Spain Sir Simon captured a Saracen. The wife of his captive came pleading for his release, bearing with her a heap of gold and jewels for his ransom.

Sir Simon was intrigued when he saw her surreptitiously rescue one little item, and demanded to see it. Most reluctantly she produced a small heart-shaped deep red jewel.

Sir Simon wanted to know why she was so anxious to keep that item out of all the lovely jewellery she was offering to redeem her husband. At long length he dragged the story out of her ..... this was a very special jewel, it had magical properties to cure men and beasts of all diseases.

That was enough for Sir Simon. He wanted it. No jewel — no husband! The Saracen woman settled for her greatest treasure — her husband!

Back home in Scotland Sir Simon had the jewel set in a coin of that age, and since then the 'Lee Penny' has been carefully cherished and guarded, and on quite a number of occasions over the centuries has been called upon to work its magic.

The Lockhard family had been well rewarded in the days of Bruce for their service to King and country,and when Sir Simon returned to Scotland with his monarch's heart, from then on the family incorporated in their arms a heart and a lock, and changed their name from Lockhard to Lockhart.

One of the family homes was at Lee castle (hence the name 'Lee Penny' for the heirloom) near Crossford in the centre of the fruit-growing district of the Clyde valley.

Ghostly royal secret of 'Tillietudlem' Castle

Perhaps a more famous castle near Crossford is Craig-nethan — better known as 'Tillietudlem' Castle. It owes its nickname to Sir Walter Scott who used Craignethan as the prototype of his 'Tillietudlem Castle' in Old Mortality, a tale of Covenanting times and the eccentric who spent his days cleaning gravestones and ensuring that the graves of fallen Covenanters were marked.

Those who haven't heard of Tillietudlem Castle in connection with Old Mortality will still recognise it from a famous Scottish song:

'Tae Tillietudlem Castle, ae summer's day I went
Tae hae a wee bit picnic and a happy day I spent ....'

Craignethan was built by the Hamiltons early in the 16th century, and, as they were strong supporters of Mary, Queen of Scots, it was to Craignethan (so it is claimed) that she was taken for safety after her escape from Lochleven Castle.

There are those, of course, who debunk Craignethan's claim to have harboured the unfortunate queen — but why then would she haunt the castle to this day? The headless lady can be nobody else but Mary who, when it was felt that a more secure place was needed, set off for Dumbarton Castle, and en route to that secure place, called at another Hamilton stronghold, Cadzow Castle; then from there, on the way to

Dumbarton, met with disaster at Langside.

The opposing forces were led by Mary's half-brother, James, Earl of Moray, who, after Mary's flight to England, had quite a few of the Hamiltons sentenced to death for treason. Pardon however was granted through the mediation of John Knox.

One of the Hamiltons however, of Bothwellhaugh, had a double grievance against Moray. Not only did he hound and persecute the Hamiltons for their support of his sister, but when he gave their estates over as forfeiture to his own cronies, one of them had been particularly cruel to Bothwellhaugh's wife, turning her out of her home with her infant, not even giving her time to dress herself or the child. So great a hardship did the poor woman suffer that night in inclement weather that she went insane and died.

Two years later Hamilton of Bothwellhaugh had his revenge when he personally assassinated Moray as he rode through Linlithgow.

Bothwellhaugh has been incorporated into the Strathclyde Regional Park along with over 1,600 acres to give the area an immense leisure park with facilities catering for all interests.

Part of the construction of this great undertaking was the diversion of the River Clyde to help form a 200-acre loch for water sports.

A little bit further down the Clyde is a place of pilgrimage for those who revere the name of David Livingstone, the great 19th century missionary explorer. Even those not very familiar with his life-story know of Henry Stanley's search for him in the African jungle and the immortal words he spoke when he finally caught up with him — 'Doctor Livingstone, I presume?'!

Livingstone was born in Blantyre on the banks of the Clyde and here the tenement in which he first saw light of day in 1813 has been converted into a memorial, which attracts thousands of visitors each year.

Just across the Clyde is Bothwell Castle, an impressive ruin of which Dorothy Wordsworth wrote, 'The castle stands nobly overlooking the Clyde.'

The poet William and his sister had been travelling around Scotland, and while William was busy composing his poems,

Dorothy was recording her own impressions of all she saw. She took a great delight in learning the history of the places she visited and, when she learned that as far back as the days of Bannockburn Bothwell had been used as a place of confinement for the prisoners of war taken in that battle, she wrote, 'If a man is to be a prisoner, he could scarcely have a more pleasant place to solace his captivity.'

But Bothwell had changed hands several times in pre-Bannockburn days. At one time the English held it and garrisoned it: then the Scots recaptured it in 1301: Edward was again on the rampage against the partisans, and to assist him in his attack on Bothwell he had made a special 'belfry' that was so huge it took 30 wagons two days to move the contraption from Glasgow to Bothwell. He thought it was worth it though — he was successful in his siege!

A leper hospital
in the Gorbals!

The 'industrial' Clyde stretches from Hamilton, Motherwell, and Wishaw, through Glasgow to Greenock.

The surrounding areas all made their contributions to making Clydeside famous the world o'er for its industry. As one Guide Book says, 'Coal from Lanarkshire's coalfields provided power for Glasgow's 19th century expansion in an era of iron and steel. Airdrie mined coal that forged Motherwell's steel, that built the ships of Clydebank.'

And in the middle of all this industry was Glasgow.

Glasgow paid a huge price for its prosperity. The 'prettiest little town' that had been so much acclaimed for its beauty in the 17th century, in the 19th century found itself gobbling up its neighbours and rivals, and, in the 20th century 'Greater Glasgow' incorporates as 'districts of Glasgow' many towns and villages of yesteryear.

For centuries Glasgow was just a backwater, of no importance, apart from its University and religious associations.

Its centre was some distance from the Clyde, in which it

was interested only as a source of water, salmon and herring. Indeed, it was so distant from the Clyde that it was deemed safe in the 14th century for a Leper Hospital to be built just across the river in the little village of Gorbals!

Lady Lochow, the benefactress who founded St Ninian's Hospital for Lepers, donated part of her lands to house the sufferers when an epidemic of the dreaded disease broke out in Glasgow.

Between two and three hundred years later it was still housing lepers, who were allowed to cross the river and beg for alms only on condition they covered their mouths, walked in the gutter and carried something to make a noise to warn folk of their presence and condition! Kindhearted folk who wanted to give them alms could do so, keeping their distance from the outcasts!

Around the little community where St Mungo served his flock was wasteland and forest, with the countryside inhabited by wolves.

One legend tells of the Bishop saint finding labour scarce at one period when he was needing some land ploughed. That posed no problem for St Mungo, however. All he had to do was to call into service two deer from the nearby woods, who were happy to oblige their friend by yoking themselves to his plough day after day ..... until a wolf attacked and killed one.

St Mungo dealt sternly with the predator. It had stopped the good work the two deer were doing — it was only just, then, that the killer should take the place of its victim!

So, the story goes, the wolf meekly lined itself up alongside the remaining deer, and together they ploughed the field until it was finished, and St Mungo, feeling the wolf had made suitable atonement, allowed it to return to the woods.

Queen Street, where British Rail now has a busy station, was, until just over 200 years ago, known as Cow Loan, for along this country lane was driven the herd of cows belonging to the inhabitants of Glasgow! The herd was the common property of the townsfolk and to look after them and take them to and from Cowcaddens each day for pasture, two men were hired as Town Herds!

The Clyde, while it supplied salmon and herring, also came in handy for dealing with women who broke the law (spiritual and temporal) — they were ducked in the river! Why the women had this extra indignity heaped upon them is not known — for, like their male counterparts, they were also put in the pillory!

Glasgow's rivals on the Clyde were Govan, Rutherglen, Renfrew and Dumbarton.

Thomas Tucker, reporting to Cromwell on the best sites for setting up Customs and Excise posts, said that Glasgow would assuredly grow 'were she not checked and kept under by the shallowness of the river.'

Being dependent on access to ports further down the Clyde was not always a good thing, as Glasgow merchants and traders found out over the centuries. On a number of occasions they had to run the picket lines set up by jealous rivals at Renfrew, Rutherglen and Dumbarton.

Glasgow's answer to this problem that reared its head from time to time was, of course to build its own port further down the Clyde and name it 'Port Glasgow'. Triumphantly the traders felt they had got the better of their rivals!

The Union of Parliaments in 1707 was opposed by Glaswegians at first — until it dawned on the traders what a vast opportunity was opening up to them to trade with the American colonies, free of restrictions.

The tobacco traders made their fortunes. Enthusiastically they expanded their trade. The 'Tobacco Lords' as they became known, became the elite of Glasgow — so much so that they reserved for themselves the privilege of walking on the 'plainstanes'. (For 'walking' read 'arrogantly strutting'.) No one else, be they female or elderly, was allowed on the pavement in the Trongate.

Dressed in their red cloaks, three-cornered hats, powdered wigs, black satin suits, silk stockings and buckled shoes, they really felt they were 'it'. They each carried a gold-topped cane — and woe betide anyone who ventured to walk where the Tobacco Lords walked! He received a resounding whack from a cane! He thought twice about trespassing again!

But with the American War of Independence trade suffered — and the Tobacco Lords' power waned.

And with the Industrial Revolution commerce in Glasgow gave way to more and more industry.

Between 1700 and 1750 Glasgow's population nearly

doubled from 12,500 to 23,000. By 1800 it was 77,000 — by 1851 it had soared to 345,000!

In the mid-nineteenth century so many people were crowded into Glasgow, working in the factories, mills and shipyards, and living in appalling conditions through overcrowding that one writer refers to it as 'the Calcutta of Europe'!

The problem was too much for the Corporation. One answer they came up with was to go round and label all the houses that had less than three rooms — the label on the outside gave the maximum number of people allowed to sleep there. Random spot checks were carried out to check for 'overcrowding'!

Prosperity, trade and industry were all thriving in Glasgow — so were slums! Glasgow grew and grew. By 1912 it had swallowed up some of its old rivals — Govan, Rutherglen and Partick.

Port Glasgow could no longer serve the needs of the rapidly expanding city. In the 18th century engineers made it possible for the Clyde to be deepened — and ships could sail right into the heart of Glasgow.

More and bigger ships meant more docks and quays. At the beginning of the 19th century Glasgow had close on 400 linear yards of quays — at the end of the century it had 14,568. All along the Clyde shipyards took over from farmlands.

But the folk who worked so hard to make Glasgow prosperous looked forward to their leisure time, short though it might be.

Factory and mill owners, shipyard bosses and other prosperous 'townees' had their holiday homes at resorts down the Clyde to which they could remove their families for the summer months while they themselves could commute either daily or weekly to keep a stringent eye on their businesses.

The poorer workers had no escape — until in 1812 Henry Bell's 'Comet' appeared on the Clyde — the forerunner of the steamers that would carry Glaswegians 'doon the watter' for their holidays or day trips, depending on which they could afford.

As they crowded the steamers to escape bustling Glasgow for the delights of Gourock, Dunoon, Rothesay or Helensburgh, the passengers passed on their way such famous works and shipyards as Harland and Wolff; Fairfields; Barclay Curle and Co.; Yarrows; John Brown's; Singer's Sewing Machine factory; Gourock Rope Works and Lithgow's.

Not that the passengers would have much chance of seeing them — at one time different steamer companies vied with each other to see which could transport their passengers in the shortest time to their destination — more often than not to the great discomfort of said passengers.

Those who could afford a few days or a week or two at the Clyde resorts had time to recover before facing the perils of the return journey, but those who were on a day trip staggered ashore to spend the first half of their day out recovering from their ordeal, and the second half trying to drum up courage for the return journey.

As the British Empire expanded, so the markets for Clydeside exports widened. Exports carried in Clydeside-built ships: liners built on the Clyde sailed to the furthest corners of the world.

And the shipyards were at their busiest when the world was at war. Ships were built, ships were repaired — at a rate of thirteen a day for five years. Little wonder Hitler sent his bombers to try to destroy Clydeside!

But in the second half of the 20th century the 'hammers' ding dong' that was 'the song of the Clyde' is muted. Glasgow and the Clyde are having to come to terms with the fact that a lot of the old traditional expertise is no longer required.

Overseas customers are supplying their own industrial needs. Modern 'container terminals' at Greenock handle cargo that Glasgow deepened its river to acccommodate. Shipyards are silent.

But Glasow is turning the ingenuity of its citizens in other directions. When the world demanded ships and steel, Glasgow gave it ships and steel.

Now the great demand is for Arts and Culture — and Glasgow is supplying that demand. Its art galleries, museums, theatres, leisure centre, parks and shops combine to offer the tourist a wealth of interest.

With the Garden Festival in 1988 and City of Culture in 1990, Glasgow proved to the world that its citizens are striving to 'Let Glasgow Flourish'.